HELP!
I'm
Married
to a
Homeschooling
MOM

HELP!
I'm Married to a
Homeschooling
MOM

Showing Dads *How to*

Meet the Needs *of* Their

Homeschooling Wives

TODD WILSON

MOODY PUBLISHERS
CHICAGO

Library of Congress Cataloging-in-Publication Data

Wilson, Todd.
  Help! I'm married to a homeschooling mom: showing dads how to meet the needs of their homeschooling wives / by Todd Wilson.
  ISBN 0-8024-2943-2
  1. Fathers—Religious life. 2. Mothers—Psychology. 3. Home schooling. 4. Husbands—Religious life. 5. Wives—Psychology. 6. Marriage—Religious aspects—Christianity. I. Title.
  BV4529.17.W56 2004
  248.8'421—dc22

                                          2003027876

1 3 5 7 9 10 8 6 4 2
Printed in the United States of America

To my lovely wife, Debbie, the mom in Help! I'm
Married to a Homeschooling Mom. *I continually thank God for the teacher He has blessed
our children with and for the partner He has
given me. You're my best friend. Thank you for
allowing me to be real about us.*

I love you,
Me

CONTENTS

INTRODUCTION

YOU'RE MARRIED TO A homeschooling mom when:

- The only time your wife looks somewhat refreshed is during the summer, two weeks at Christmas, and one week during the spring.
- Your wife's eyes light up when you say the words "curriculum fair."
- Your wife's idea of a romantic getaway involves 6,000 other people, workshops, and hundreds of book vendors.
- You give your wife a love note, and she grades it.
- Your wife weeps every time a school bus drives by.
- Your wife prays every night for the Lord to return before the next day of school.
- Instead of, "Not now, I have a headache," your wife says, "Not now, I have to go over my lesson plan."
- Your wife "scolds" in her sleep.
- You've eaten cereal for dinner sometime this past week.

- The first place you look for your wife when you come home from work is in the closet.
- Your wife will only talk to you if you raise your hand.
- Your wife talks with telemarketers for the adult conversation.

It doesn't matter what the experts say. I know for a fact that one of the toughest jobs on earth is being a homeschooling mom. Who else is expected to prepare lesson plans for three different age groups, teach complex problems to small humans who pick their noses, and referee pint-sized preschoolers who fight over toys, all at the same time?

A homeschooling mom is responsible for all her children's learning and running a household. There are dishes to wash, rooms to clean, meals to cook, and a husband to clean up after. If—and it's a big if—she has any energy left, she is expected to "never let [her] man forget he's a man."

TOUGHER YET

But, as difficult as it is being a homeschooling mom, it's even tougher being married to a homeschooling mom. Instead of being greeted by a put-together woman resembling June Cleaver, the husband of a homeschooling mom is met by a woman who looks like a serial killer waiting for another victim.

The unsuspecting husband naively offers his great wisdom in response to her terrible day, but that only adds fuel to a fire that is already burning out of control.

"I forgot to thaw the meat," she says while looking at her husband like it's his fault. "You got any ideas for dinner?"

Jim knew this was bad. The home atmosphere
alert had been rasied to **defcon 4.**

Without thinking, he offers, "Why don't you cook up some of your world famous lasagna. It's not that hard, is it?"

She rolls her eyes in disgust and estimates that it will take two hours to get it on the table.

"That's okay, Dear," he reassures her, patting her shoulder. "That will give me time to read the paper. It's been a tough day. Besides, I ate a late lunch at Applebee's with some of the guys."

The next thing he knows, lasagna noodles are dripping from his head.

"What? Did I say something wrong?" he asks.

TWO ARE BETTER THAN ONE

Dad, I applaud you for giving your family the privilege of being educated at home, and I sympathize with your plight of being married to a homeschooling mom. However, if you expect your wife to successfully pull off this homeschooling task, then she's going to need your help.

Homeschooling is a tremendous undertaking. It can crush a woman who is forced to carry it alone. Homeschooling is at its best when the husband and wife shoulder its weight. Working as a team doesn't make it easy—that would be wishful thinking—but it does make it easier.

Together, you can do almost anything. And with God's help and strength, you can do all things (Philippians 4:13). When the tough days come (which in my household is about every third day), you can weather them together. When one of you starts to have second thoughts or doubts, the other one comes to the rescue. If you both start to wilt, then together you hang on to God until the fatigue passes.

Husband, your wife longs to have you as her partner, like a person crawling through the desert longs for water. She was created to have you at her side, defending, supporting, and leading her.

Unfortunately, most women embark on the homeschooling journey alone. They pick out the curriculum, do the lesson plans, teach the kids, and juggle all the demands of running a house. They walk the earth like the living dead. The joy that they once exuded is a foggy memory. They get cranky with you, the kids, and the dog.

Introduction

LOWER YOUR EXPECTATIONS

Are you one of those dads who set incredibly high expectations? Do you get concerned if eight-year-old Copernicus (homeschoolers hardly ever choose normal names) isn't reading at a college level, and wonder why the house isn't as clean as it once was?

Your unrealistic expectations, disapproval, and lack of interest further the burnout of your homeschooling wife until she's ready to throw in the towel.

What your wife really needs is your help.

You may not be able to do much of the teaching, but there are many other ways in which you can help. The whole family benefits when you pitch in because when mama's happy, everyone's happy.

Eleven of the next twelve chapters discuss the different needs of your homeschooling wife that you can meet (and only the last chapter is devoted to your needs).

My desire is not to pistol-whip you into submission. I simply want you and your wife to make it to the end of your homeschooling adventure in one piece, having enjoyed the ride together.

CHAPTER ONE

Your WIFE
Needs: YOUR
HELP

"Two are better than one, because they have a good return for their work: If [a homeschooling wife] falls down, [her husband] can help [her] up. But pity the [homeschooling mom] who falls and has no one to help [her] up!"

❖ ECCLESIASTES 4:9–10

WHAT I PICTURED when we decided to home-school was a whole lot prettier than it actually is. I envisioned my children sitting quietly at wooden school desks while my wife taught them. They would start the day in prayer, read wonderful literature, and cut pumpkins out of orange construction paper.

With me as the principal (which meant that I didn't have to do anything), I'd be a respected figurehead and receive an occasional progress report. Most of the time, I would reign from my office.

At the end of each workday, I would return home to a spotless house, where my wife would stop in the midst of the home-cooked meal preparation to greet me. The children

A really dumb question

would run to hug their old man, and I would sit around basking in the glory of the thought that "we" were preparing our children for the real world.

Then, reality hit. I realized that there was a lot of work for me, too! I thought it was "a wife thing" and that my life would stay pretty normal. Now I know that the only way to make it work is for it to be "a husband and wife thing." And now it's clear that my life is anything but normal.

ME, TEACH?

It's not realistic to assume that every husband can help teach his children, but that doesn't let you off the hook. There is no reason why you can't be involved in the teaching and training of your children. Remember, it's not just your wife's job.

There are certain subjects that are easier for you to teach than they are for your wife. In my house, I'm the creative one, and my wife is the methodical number cruncher. She doesn't like crafts, but I do. So I do a craft with the kids every once in a while. She likes English, literature, and math. She teaches those subjects since I can barely count with my fingers and toes.

You might like teaching history, Bible, or science. Whatever your gift is—use it. If you work an odd shift, offer to teach one morning a week or to take the kids on an educational outing. Grade papers, listen to kids read, help with science projects, drill with flashcards, or take a trip to the library.

NO PAIN, NO GAIN

Even if you aren't able to share the teaching responsibilities, you can help in other ways. These sting a little more, but they are just as helpful. Housework. Yeah, you read that right —housework. You know—vacuuming, dusting, straightening, or even doing dishes.

When you do the dishes, your wife doesn't have to. When you vacuum, your wife doesn't have to. When you give baths, she doesn't have to.

"Yeah, but, I won't have as much time to work out, watch sports, be involved at church, or restore my 1956 Corvette," you argue.

Exactly. That's part of homeschooling. If you really believe in homeschooling, then you must be willing to make some sacrifices. Your wife does every day.

DOING MY DUTY

I've taken it upon myself to help ease my wife's load. She didn't ask me, beg me, or threaten to quit if I didn't pitch in. I'm committed to what we're doing, and I want to prove it. One of the areas in which I've chosen to concentrate my efforts is the homeschool room. It's in our attic, and every day by the time school is over, it looks as if a tornado swept through.

I realized that it would be helpful to my wife to start each school day with a clean schoolroom. My plan was to have the kids and me straighten it up every night before going to bed.

In theory, it was a simple and relatively pain-free way to show my dedication to homeschooling. In reality, it's just plain hard work. I've climbed those steps many times and prayed, "Dear God, please let it be mostly clean."

I'm not sure that He has ever answered that prayer.

But I keep praying, and I keep cleaning.

WANT TO HEAR A SECRET?

Dad, here's a secret. I hate straightening up the homeschool room. I hate doing the dishes. I'd much rather be doing what I want to do than to be giving our kids baths and cleaning up the family room.

But, I am committed to homeschooling, and I love my wife. I know that if she is to do most of what homeschooling involves, then I'm going to have to do some things that I hate doing. In fact, in some twisted way, I am glad to do them, because I know I'm helping her.

It's true—I won't be able to do all that I want to do. I won't be able to have abs of steel, a golf score that would make Tiger Woods jealous, or watch every ballgame during the season, but that's the choice I made when we started this adventure. Sacrifice leads to successful homeschooling in the long run.

So, put aside the newspaper, turn off the TV, roll up your sleeves, and get to work.

NO PARADES

Here's one last helpful hint: Don't expect any parades. What I mean by that is, don't expect your wife to jump up and down every time you do a little housework.

Bill was setting himself up for a disappointment.

I confess that was the reason behind some of my "do gooding." I did the dishes, and then when my wife failed to acknowledge the job, I said something like, "Hey, I took it upon myself to do the dishes . . . I hope it's all right."

When she failed to praise me for my selfless giving, I was a little more straightforward (and mean). "You're welcome for doing the dishes," I said.

She looked at me, having cleaned the kitchen a thousand times without any acknowledgment, and said with a smile, "Don't expect any parades."

So, Dad, when you ease the burden from your beloved bride's shoulders, don't expect a celebration in your honor.

Twenty practical ways you can help your wife:

1. run errands

2. go to the grocery store

3. do laundry

4. dust

5. clean tubs and showers

6. give baths

7. wash dishes

8. replace burned-out lightbulbs

9. balance the checkbook

10. make sure her car is gassed up

11. answer the phone

12. get up in the middle of the night to meet the needs of a child

13. pay bills

14. pick up the kids and the dry cleaning

15. take the responsibility for any problems (car/utilities/repairs)

16. do the banking

17. straighten up the house at the end of the day

18. get breakfast for the kids

19. empty the dishwasher

20. read to the kids

Your WIFE
Needs: YOUR
ENCOURAGEMENT

*"[Homeschooling moms and dads] encourage
one another daily, as long as it is called Today."*

❖ HEBREWS 3:13

DURING THE SUMMER of 1996, all eyes were
glued to the television set for the final round of women's
gymnastics. It was a battle between petite gladiators for the
all-around gold, and it was down to two teams: America
and Russia.

The last event determined the gold and the silver. Both
teams performed spectacularly. The last event, the vault,
was up, where one step backward could result in defeat.

Kerri Strug, at 4 feet 9 1/2 inches tall, stepped to the
line. Her eyes blazed with determination as she stared down
the lane. The pressure of the moment weighed heavily upon
her, but she was up to the challenge.

With a deep breath, she rocked back, sprinted down the
path, hit the horse, spun into the air, and landed in a bone-
crunching heap on the mat with a scream. She had badly

injured her ankle. Her thick-accented coach raced to her side as the crowd gasped at the horrible timing.

THE REST OF THE STORY

Kerri Strug was out, and the Americans had lost—at least that's what everyone thought. A deafening cheer erupted ten minutes later, when Kerri hobbled to the line with a heavily bandaged ankle and tears in her eyes.

The crowd stared in disbelief. How could she endure the pain of another run, let alone the landing? It was insane. But she did it! She stuck the landing and hobbled to the platform with her teammates to receive the gold medal.

Somehow, she had done the impossible.

I believe the reason for her success was her coach who stood on the sidelines repeating, "You can do it, Kerri! You can do it!" He didn't tell her how or why; he just told her she could do it—and she did.

YOU CAN DO IT!

Mark Twain once said he could live for a week on a single compliment. It could be said of a homeschooling wife that she can teach for 180 days on a good supply of encouragement.

Your wife wants what everyone wants—an encourager. She needs you to stand alongside her and tell her often, "You can do it! YOU CAN DO IT!!!"

That can be done through appreciation notes tucked into lesson plans, a bouquet of flowers sent to the house for "the world's best teacher," or the simple praise of a man who is grateful for all the work his wife does to educate the children.

Praise her through the good times and encourage her through the bad. Snuggle up to her in bed at night and whisper in her ear, "You're doing a great job." Let her know that you realize that the task is difficult and that you thank God that she is your wife and your children's teacher.

When she feels unable to start the day, say, *"You can do it!"*

When she isn't sure which curriculum to pick, say, *"I believe in you!"*

When she isn't sure if she is doing a good job, say, *"You're doing great!"*

And when she is ready to throw in the towel, say, *"We need you."*

Cheer her on often, and you will both stand on the platform to receive the gold.

The homeschooling decorator

Ideas for encouraging your home-schooling wife:

- Brag about her when you are in a group (especially when she's with you).
- When you pray at the dinner table, thank God (out loud) for your children's good teacher.
- On National Teacher's Appreciation Day (May 6) celebrate with cake, dinner out, or a gift.
- Leave an apple on her desk with a mushy (no pun intended) note attached.
- On the first day of school, surprise her with a bouquet of flowers or some fun teaching supplies.
- Drop her a note requesting a romantic parent/teacher conference.
- Write a message on a sticky-note thanking her for all that she does. Place it on her lesson plan or her toothbrush.
- Pick up something special for her on your way home from work.
- Call her from work just to express your thankfulness.
- If she's having a tough day, have something delivered to the house.
- Insist that she go out with a friend for dinner or dessert while you watch the kids.
- Buy her a card and write something personal on the inside. For example, you could write "You're My Hero" and list the reasons behind the statement.

CHAPTER THREE

Your WIFE
Needs: YOUR
LEADERSHIP

"Love the LORD your God with all your heart and with all your soul and with all your strength. These commandments that I give you today are to be upon your hearts. Impress them on your children. Talk about them when you sit at home and when you walk along the road, when you lie down and when you get up."

❖ DEUTERONOMY 6:5–7

You are the head of your family, the king of the castle, the captain of the ship. To some that looks like a job of a person who is highly celebrated, but we know better—it's not. It's a bum deal most of the time. If you're like me, you get tired of taking all the blame, and every once in a while, you'd like to pass the buck to someone else.

But since it's God's idea, you're stuck with it. To be the head means you're responsible. You're responsible for the household's safety, tangible needs, spiritual training, and (gulp) education.

Repeat after me, "I am responsible for the education of my children." Again. Louder. Taste the words in your mouth and get used to them.

TO LEAD OR NOT TO LEAD

One of the best ways to encourage your wife is to take the lead in educating your children. It's one thing to be in favor of homeschooling; it's another thing altogether to take the lead in homeschooling.

Ask most men why they homeschool, and they'll answer, "Because my wife wants to." That's an answer, but it's not a very good one, because one day the tired wife will change her mind, and then what?

She'll look to her husband for answers and support. All he'll do is shrug his shoulders and say, "I guess it's up to you."

What our wives need is a "lead dog."

THE LEAD DOG

Perhaps you've seen a movie with this kind of scenario . . . A man is trekking across a frozen wasteland in a desperate struggle to get from point A to point B. The dogs bark and tug at their lines, pulling the sled that is loaded down with medical provisions to save a dying community.

The Eskimo stops the sled and walks along the line of dogs to get to the lead dog that stands alone in front. He leans down and talks to him about the graveness of the mission (as if the dog can understand him) and returns to his position.

With a crack of the whip, the dogs begin to pull, led by the lead dog. They count on him. He doesn't pull any harder or get more food at the end. He just receives his instruction from the master, leads the others, and gives direction.

Dad, you are that dog. Your wife is counting on you to lead and so is God. Leadership comes with a price. If there

After Johnson spoke, they knew that they had been topped.

is a problem with the dogs pulling the sled, the lead dog is the one who feels the tip of the whip. He is responsible, and so are you. So if there is a problem in your homeschool or your wife is frustrated with the kids, then it's your responsibility to fix it.

GOOD QUESTION

As the lead dog, you have to know where you're going, why you're going there, and how you plan to get there. You need to know the reason for home educating your children. When you're in a group and someone asks why you homeschool, your wife shouldn't have to think about what she is going to say, because you should have an answer ready.

When she looks at you with tears in her eyes, convinced

that she is ruining the children and doing a terrible job, you must remind her why you decided to homeschool in the first place.

There are as many reasons for homeschooling as there are homeschoolers. Some families homeschool to give their kids a better education. Some want to stress the basics, while others want to teach classic languages.

Some homeschoolers came out of a public school setting and are determined to protect their children from that environment. Others want to play an active role in giving their children a biblical worldview since they won't be taught that in a public school.

Still others are doing it for financial reasons. They don't want to put their kids in public school and can't afford private school.

And I suppose there are some who just like the idea of teaching their kids, day in and day out, working themselves to the bone, while surrounded by runny-nosed kids.

The truth is that most people homeschool for a variety of different reasons. Take us, for example.

OUR STORY

When we were fresh out of the starting blocks as parents, we assumed we'd send our kids off to public school. My wife attended a Christian school, and I attended a small-town public school. Both of us had good experiences plus a few experiences we wanted our kids to bypass.

We didn't have much of a plan. We just assumed that our kids would do what most kids in America do. They'd reach a certain age, and then we'd stick them on a bus only to see them a few hours later after they got their "book learning."

But our plans began to change as our children grew older. We opened our eyes to see the other kids that would become their school peers. We gulped in fear.

We saw kids who came from broken homes, drug-using homes, godless homes, foul-talking homes, and we were not about to surround our naive children with those kinds of influences. And that's not even mentioning the anti-Christian teaching they would receive in some of their classes.

Some people would argue that we are to be salt and light in the dark world—which is true—but nowhere are we told to subject our kids to utter darkness. In fact, we believe that our job as parents is to prepare our children to be salt and light. But if the salt loses its saltiness (even at a young age), then it is worthless and unusable (see Matthew 5:13).

It's like preparing soldiers for battle. When a new recruit enlists, he isn't immediately given a uniform, a gun, and sent to the front lines. That would be suicide and would lead to defeat. Instead, the soldier trains for months until he is ready for battle. We believe it is our job as parents to prepare our children for the battle and not stick them in the heat of it until they're prepared. If we stick them in too soon—they'll lose.

So it was settled. We would send our kids to a private, Christian school where godly people would educate them and they'd be surrounded by other kids from godly families. It didn't matter that we would have to sell the house and live in a cardboard box under a bridge to afford it—we were committed to raising godly children after all.

We had a plan.

Then something happened along the way. We opened our eyes and saw that some of the kids that we worried would poorly influence our children were Christian-school kids.

We didn't want to be judgmental, because we knew a lot of good, godly Christian parents who sent their kids to Christian school. That wasn't the problem.

The problem was those other families who were simply trying to get their kids out of the public school and into a better, safer environment.

Even as young parents, we knew that kids "rise" to the lowest level. Take a room full of decent kids and introduce one disobedient, foul-talking child and guess who they emulate?

Yep.

It's a kid thing. Not only that, but it's a biblical thing. "Do not be misled: 'Bad company corrupts good character'" (1 Corinthians 15:33). We realized that our kids would be best off at home, with their brothers and sisters as peers rather than twenty other kids.

That left us with two choices. Forget schooling altogether or educate our children at home.

I was for the first one, but I listened to the wisdom of my wife, and we chose the second option. We knew very little about homeschooling, except our reasons for doing it:

1. To protect our children from ungodly, worldly influences.
2. To train our children to influence the world for Christ.
3. To teach our children to love God with all their hearts at all times.

Those reasons have been our solid ground because, like every other homeschooling mom, my wife has doubts. She often thinks she's failing our children by not giving them the education that they need.

I sit next to her on our bed as she cries about how hard it is and threatens to quit. If I'm being a good husband, I let her cry and empathize with her about the difficult path we've chosen. Then I remind her why we've chosen this path . . . We get to be the ones to train and prepare our children for what lies ahead. They are good friends with one another, and in elementary school they are playing together with Legos, instead of hearing from other kids about preteen girls getting pregnant. At this point, my wife usually sniffs back the last few tears, nods her head in agreement, and we keep moving forward.

The world meets a homeschooler

WHAT'S YOUR STORY?

So, Dad, what's your story? What's your solid ground? What are your reasons for doing what you do? If you don't really know why you're homeschooling, then take the lead and together, with your wife, find out. There are several books listed below that can help.

Once you've decided, stick to the high ground and don't look back or around to see what everyone else is doing. The world may not understand, but that's okay. Your extended family may not understand, but that's okay too. In fact, other believers in your church may not understand.

What they think doesn't matter. Just keep your eyes on the Master and pull with all your might. Never forget that you're the lead dog, and they're counting on you.

KEEP THE TROOPS INFORMED

Not only is it important for you to know the reasons behind your decision to homeschool, but it is also important for your children to know the reasons. Occasionally, they might get "the question." Other kids will ask them where they go to school, and their friends will talk about how great it is to be at a "real school."

I'll never forget the day that our oldest son, Ben, asked us after being homeschooled for four years, "So why do people homeschool? I mean, why do we homeschool?" I knew then that we had let him down by failing to share our vision with him.

If your kids have no idea why they are taught at home, frustration and exasperation can occur. They might ask, "Why can't we go to a real school like our friends?"

"Because I said so", isn't good enough. Instead, give them real reasons for your decision. Tell them why you believe so strongly in home education. Don't come across as judgmental of others, but let them know that you're only doing it because you love them so much and you think it's best.

Kids can deal with that. They may not always like it, but they can deal with it. As they grow up, they'll respect you for going against the flow and doing what is best for them.

Resources for the "why" behind homeschooling:

Card, Susan, and Michael Card. *The Homeschool Journey* (Eugene, OR: Harvest House Publishing, 1997).

Klicka, Christopher. *The Right Choice: The Incredible Failure of Public Education and the Rising Hope of Home Schooling* (Gresham, OR: Noble Books, 1994).

MacAulay, Susan Schaeffer. *For the Children's Sake* (Wheaton, IL: Good News Publishers, 1984).

Quine, David, and Shirley Quine. *Let Us Highly Resolve* (Richardson, TX: Cornerstone Curriculum Project, 1999).

CHAPTER FOUR

Your WIFE Needs: YOUR LISTENING EAR

"[A homeschooling husband] who answers before listening—that is his folly and his shame."

❖ PROVERBS 18:13

TIM ALLEN SPENT several years poking fun of men on his weekly sitcom *Home Improvement*. During one memorable episode, he and a couple of his belching buddies sat around exchanging stories about how they never listen to their wives.

It went something like this:

"The other night," one of the guys bragged, "my wife asked me about putting new drapes in the sun room . . . I didn't even know we had a sun room!" Laughter erupted.

"Oh, yeah," another guy added, "my wife started talking about decorating the living room, and I was clinically dead for three minutes." More laughter.

Then Tim threw in his two cents. "I've got it all figured out. Whenever my wife starts talking, I just nod my head and say, 'Uh huh . . . uh huh.'" More laughter.

Moments before the big blowout

The conversation got videotaped, and Tim's wife saw the tape. You can imagine the rest of the show.

Men all across America laughed when they saw the episode, and wives rolled their eyes because they knew all too well that this sort of thing happens. We men don't listen to our wives enough. To be more specific, we husbands of homeschooling wives don't always listen when they need to talk. We nod our heads and say, "Uh huh," but our brains go south for the winter.

YOU'RE NOT LISTENING

What really gets me is that my wife knows when I'm not listening. I get that glazed look in my eyes and my nonverbal cues shout, "I'm bored."

Not long ago, we were having a conversation, when she

suddenly stopped mid-sentence and said, "You're not listening to me."

"Yes, I am," I said, but she knew I wasn't.

It's not that I find my wife boring. I just don't always like discussing the pros and cons of different math programs. Why does it matter whether we use Miquon, Saxon, or Bob Jones? Aren't numbers just numbers? As far as I'm concerned, the kids can just count on their fingers and toes. I don't care which math program she chooses, just as long as she picks one!

What I conveyed to my wife that night was that I didn't care about her. Because if I care about my wife, then what she cares about ought to be important to me because she is important to me.

You don't have to become an expert in all areas of home-schooling, but you do need to listen and talk over options. The temptation for me is to listen quickly and then give an off-the-cuff answer like, "Sure, honey, I'd go with that Miquon whatchamacallit program. So are we done?"

We usually are, but only because she left the room.

My wife wants me to listen and think over the options with her, weigh them carefully (thinking of all the pros and cons), and imagine all the possible cataclysmic, world problems that will result if the wrong option is chosen.

There I go again.

IT EVEN WORKS WITH SOCKS

It's the same story when my wife is trying to choose which socks to wear. She knows what blouses look good with what pants and what shoes go with what skirts. That's why it boggles my mind when she asks my advice on any clothing combination. If my clothes match, it's by accident, and when

I dress the kids for church, they look like street urchins.

When we were first married, we were in our bedroom getting dressed for something where we needed to look good. All of a sudden, my wife walked out of the closet holding her pant legs up and asked, "Which socks do you think go better with these pants?"

I looked at her like she was crazy.

"Why does it matter which socks you wear? No one's going to see your socks anyway."

An icy chill crept over the room, and I knew I had said the wrong thing. What I had conveyed to my wife was that not only were socks unimportant to me, but so was she.

So, months later when she stepped out of the closet and asked the question again, I paused, remembering the last instance, pointed to one leg and said, "I'd wear those."

She looked up at me like I had done something terrible and said, "You didn't even think about the choices."

I looked at her and said rather loudly, "What does it matter? They're only socks!"

That icy chill crept over the room, again. I had muffed it once more.

So, now when she stands before me and asks my opinion about socks, I pause and look at her feet thoughtfully.

"Turn around," I say, carefully weighing the decision. "I'd definitely go with the one on the right."

She smiles and then chooses the one on the left, but she feels cared about, and that's what every wife wants.

A GOOD EXAMPLE

A good example of how listening works is the brother-in-law example. I heard it from my wife, who heard it from her sister. Apparently my sister-in-law was feeling overwhelmed and discouraged, and she needed to talk. She asked her husband if he would spend the evening talking through all her concerns—and he did.

They talked for a couple of hours, and in her own words she later told my wife, "I felt so refreshed and ready to go after talking to him. It made such a big difference." Wow, talk about scoring a three-pointer. He proved to his wife that homeschooling was important to him by listening. Consequently, she felt cared about. BINGO!

SHOW YOU CARE

When your wife wants to talk, listen. When she needs your opinion, give her yours. When it's time for the annual homeschool convention, go with her. No excuses.

If you need to find someone to watch the kids, then do it. Sit through the seminars, and plan to spend countless hours going up and down the aisles of curriculum vendors. Okay, it's about as fun as watching paint dry, but go anyway.

Be interested, and when your wife asks your opinion about two or three products, listen thoughtfully, ask questions, and help her make a decision.

Of course, she won't decide then, because she'll need to stop at every other booth to compare products in hopes of saving two dollars. But by the end of the day, she'll know that you're on the same team.

TWO HEADS ARE BETTER THAN ONE

Everyone knows that two heads are better than one. Your involvement provides the extra brain. You may see problems that your wife doesn't. You may have insights about handling issues that have her perplexed, or you may spot pitfalls that have gone unnoticed by her.

God knew best when He created a man and a woman. You need your wife as much as she needs you. If you don't contribute, or you just nod your head and say, "Uh huh," then your wife is forced to walk the path alone.

HOMEWORK

Tonight, ask your wife what the hardest part of her home-school day is and then listen. Don't rush in and try to solve everything. Just ask questions and let her talk. It may take a couple of hours, so don't make any plans for the evening, but it will be worth it.

Oh, and compliment her on the details, like her socks.

CHAPTER FIVE

Your WIFE Needs: YOUR MUSCLE

*"Husbands, in the same way be considerate as you
live with your [homeschooling] wives, and treat
them with respect as the weaker partner and as
heirs with you of the gracious gift of life, so that
nothing will hinder your prayers."*

❖ 1 PETER 3:7

WHETHER YOUR WIFE WANTS to admit it or
not, she is the weaker partner. Picture an exquisite, fragile
work of art, like a cut glass vase, the kind that will shatter into
a million pieces if handled harshly, and that's the idea behind
the word "weaker."

God created the homeschooling wife to be cherished and
nurtured. She may not like it, and society is doing everything it can to change that perception, but it's still the truth.

FRAGILE MEANS HANDLE WITH CARE

Know what? Men prefer fragile vessels. Who wouldn't
choose a cut glass vase over a plastic Tupperware pitcher? One
is special and the other is treated like, well, plastic Tupperware.

We want our wives to need us, depend on us, and be like damsels in distress waiting for us to rescue them.

And yet, the only time that we don't like them to be fragile vessels is when they are acting especially fragile. It throws us off when they burst into tears and cry for no apparent reason. It's so . . . womanlike.

As men, we jump in and try to solve the problems, but usually that just causes more tears because she does not feel understood.

When your wife becomes frustrated over little things, you'll complain to yourself and God, wishing that she would buck up and be tougher. You fail to remember that the reason she is acting weaker is because she is weaker.

Your wife's weakness requires a gentle respect. Otherwise, you want her to be something she isn't, and the Bible says that your prayers are hindered. Although I don't know what

that means entirely, I do know that your relationship with God is negatively impacted when you mistreat your wife.

Think about the implications: When you treat your wife like Tupperware, your prayers are hindered. Which means, you're wasting your time praying until you start protecting, encouraging, and caring for your homeschooling wife.

SHOW YOUR MUSCLE

Even if it goes against your nature, allow your wife to cry. Don't try to resolve everything, and don't scold her for feeling a certain way. Listen to her talk, and empathize with her. Pray with her and for her.

If one of your children is being extra difficult, then step in and deal with that child. If your wife is overwhelmed with the hundred-plus choices of curriculum, then spend time pouring over the pages with her until one is chosen. If her schedule isn't working, then help her come up with one that will work for her.

If she feels scrutinized by your parents or hers for homeschooling, then take it upon yourself to take the heat and talk with them. You are her knight in shining armor, her defender, and her strength. She wants to lean upon you and rest in your arms. She is weaker and knows it (even though she may not admit it). She needs you.

As John Wayne used to do in the old westerns, you need to saddle up to your weaker vessel and say, "Come on over here little lady, and I'll take care of ya."

Women would love husbands like that.

THE FAMILY POWWOW

I've already said that you're responsible for the success

or failure of your homeschool. There will be times when you'll need to flex your muscle to address specific problems.

In my family, I know it's time for a family meeting when my wife threatens to quit and put the kids up for sale. The sparkle in her eyes is gone, and she sighs a lot.

As dinner is about to wrap up, I announce that there will be a family meeting after the meal. Immediately, the kids know that something is up because Dad has called a family meeting.

With the dishes still on the table, we all gather in the family room and the meeting starts. I'm in charge, and I ask the questions.

"How are things going in school?" I ask my wife so everyone can hear her response.

Calmly, she begins to lay out her grievances. The kids start to squirm.

"Yeah, but Katherine . . . " one of them starts.

I raise a single finger to quiet the interrupter. This is Mom's time to talk. I listen and ask a few questions of the kids, and together we talk through some of our options.

Basically, there are two options: One brings pleasure, the other brings pain.

We talk some more about the purpose of our family and homeschooling, we pray, and the troops are dismissed.

Life looks pretty much the same after the meeting, but beneath the surface a lot has taken place. First, I have exercised my authority as the father and reminded my kids that when things go wrong they'll have to deal with me. Second, it gives me an accurate picture of what has been going on during school that I may not know about.

Third, it lets all family members express their concerns and frustrations. Sometimes by just talking about the problems, a solution presents itself that would have gone overlooked had the problem not been aired.

Lastly, my wife sees my commitment to what we are doing. There is safety and security knowing that I'm in the driver's seat, that I'll step up to the plate when needed to, and that I am loved for doing so.

You will be, too.

CHAPTER SIX

Your WIFE Needs: YOUR MONEY

> *"One [homeschooling husband] gives freely, yet gains even more; another withholds unduly, but comes to poverty."*
>
> ✣ PROVERBS 11:24

I PROBABLY DON'T NEED to tell you that homeschooling ain't cheap. Thankfully, I have a wife who tries to keep costs down, but when I see her eyeing a $50 book, I get a lump in my throat the size of a turnip.

When she reads off a list of books that she plans to buy, my brain kicks into autopilot, and I say things like, "Is the library closed? I'm pretty sure they'd have all the books on that list, and they're FREE."

She argues the fact that it's not always convenient to lug five kids to the library and spend time searching for the list of books she needs. She also adds that she wants to build up our own family library to give the kids a constant supply of good character-building books, and that it's just easier to buy them.

A homeschool dad and his money are soon parted.

But the "cheapskate battle" doesn't end there. There are still curriculums to buy, accessories to purchase, and learning tools to obtain. With each box that shows up at our front door, I hear the "ker-ching" of a cash register.

I'M CHEAP

I try to hide the fact that I'm cheap—no, frugal. After all, I want to give my wife the freedom to buy the best tools for the job, but I usually end up blowing it.

For example: Not long ago, we were sitting on the couch talking about the merits and drawbacks of two particular curriculums. I could tell which one she was leaning toward, but I had one more question to ask before I gave my final opinion.

"So, how much do they cost?" I asked, pretending like it didn't really matter.

She looked at the book list and answered, "This one is $120 and . . . this one is $35."

No brainer. "Well, you know . . . I think maybe that one (the $35 one) looks like a better program. It might be a ton more work, but I, uh, think it looks better, yeah, better." And I wondered if she saw through my cleverly conceived strategy.

She obviously did, because she ended up buying the more expensive program, which is, I might add, the better program.

Unfortunately, I act cheap—frugal—at curriculum fairs, Wal-Mart, K-Mart, and everywhere else that products are sold. My wife holds up two items, I ask how much they cost, and then I always pick the cheaper. Then I usually experience a sudden change in climate (if you know what I mean).

THE $1.39 LESSON

My frugality was first pointed out to me within the first couple months of our marriage. My wife and I were standing in line at a fast food restaurant when my wife spotted a large poster advertising a banana milkshake. Banana is one of her favorite flavors, and she announced cheerfully, "I think I'll get a banana milkshake."

I glanced at the poster and saw the price cleverly tucked away near the bottom of the poster: $1.39. My cheap part of the brain started to reel at the expense.

"Sure," I countered, "if you get water instead of a soft drink." After all, I thought everyone knew that you'd never get a shake and a soft drink.

It took about four seconds before I knew that I had done something wrong.

What I conveyed to my wife on that hot summer day was that she wasn't worth $1.39 to me.

It's the same message I convey when I choose a $35 math program over a much better $120 program just because of the price tag.

GOOD TOOLS

Most men like good tools. I like the feel of a well-made tool in my hand. Its cold, machined steel is calibrated to within thousandths of an inch. Perfection.

Unfortunately, most of my good tools have been either pounded into the ground or left out in the rain by one of my children, only to be discovered when I ran over them with my mower.

So instead of using good tools, I either dig into my wife's pink toolbox for a pink handled screwdriver or borrow one of my kids' fifty-cent wrenches.

The other day, I needed a socket wrench. Unable to find mine, I borrowed my son Ben's that clicked both ways. Talk about frustration. It took me three times as long as it should have to do the simple job I was working on.

That's what happens when you use cheap tools, because the expensive truth is: Good tools get the job done easier and better. And Dad, that goes with homeschooling tools as well as your tools.

THE PRICE OF HOMESCHOOLING

Although spending money is hard for me, I want my wife to know that I'm behind her in what she is doing. Part of that backing comes from paying for the tools she needs to do the job. I know that a more expensive tool usually makes completion of the work smoother, better, and easier.

I "know" these things, but I don't always "feel" them. But the way I look at it is, if I'm committed to homeschooling then I'm going to go with what I know and not what I feel. When she announces that she is buying an expensive book filled with incredible illustrations, I will respond with, "That sounds great. The kids will love it."

When she holds up two choices, I will ask a lot of questions, the cost not being one of them.

LET'S GO OUT TO EAT

Another thing that might involve spending money when you homeschool is going out to eat. I know of a few guys who do the cooking at their house. It's a huge help to their wives. But since I'm no chef, I do the next best thing.

When I come home and find a large, still-frozen block of meat sitting on the kitchen counter and a crazed look in my wife's eyes, I announce: "We're going out tonight."

As the words leave my mouth, a wave of relief washes over my wife and she smiles.

"We shouldn't eat out or spend the money," she says, looking every bit like a schoolgirl who has just been asked out.

Now, if I'm being especially stupid, I might think about what she says and respond, "Well, that's true . . . maybe we should eat at home."

Suddenly, a cold wave drenches her countenance, leaving a disappointed person in its wake.

So instead, when my wife says that we don't have to go out to eat, I respond with, "Oh, who cares, you know we only live once." The smile remains, she feels cared about, and I realize that it was the best investment that I could have made.

There are some men, however, who basically refuse to go out for dinner.

"I eat lunch out everyday at work, and I want a home cooked meal," they argue, having forgotten about their commitment to homeschooling.

You want a real eye opener? Try homeschooling for a week. Then you'll beg to eat out just to get out of the house.

So, on those days that you are greeted at the door by a zombie-eyed wife who has no idea what to fix for dinner and no energy left to make it, offer to take the family out to eat.

OTHER HIDDEN COSTS

There are some other hidden costs that arise. Some are: retreats for your wife, field trips and outings, date nights, and other tools that make the job of homeschooling easier.

A homeschooling mom's field of dreams

If you can afford it, hire someone to come in and clean the house once a week. One dad hired a maid to come in and clean their house so his wife could concentrate on homeschooling their children.

I love his explanation. "I figured I'd rather pay someone to clean our house so my wife can teach our kids at home than pay someone else to teach our kids so my wife can clean our home."

Well said, Dad!

Another dad hired a young woman to come in a few days a week to help with their four small children. Now that's a man who stands behind his homeschooling wife.

BUDGET IT

For some of you, the word "budget" is a pleasant word. But if you're like me, then the word "budget" brings to mind images of chains and captivity. But I've learned that by budgeting for books and curriculum, I give my wife the freedom to buy what she needs, and it allows us to save for the big expenses, making the $246 purchase of literature books easier to swallow.

My wife has friends who often say: "I don't know what to do about this subject for next year because my husband says we can't spend any money on that right now." It doesn't have to be that way.

Map out what your wife needs per year for homeschooling curriculum, and then break that down to what you need to save per month. If your wife does a lot of one-stop shopping and big homeschool purchases all at once, you can set aside savings so that at the end of the year, your wife has all the money she needs for the next school year.

If you don't think there's room to add anything else to the monthly budget, then think of areas you can cut back. There aren't many things more important than raising and educating your children. Perhaps you can cut out monthly cable bills, magazine subscriptions, unnecessary phone features, or pack your lunch instead of eating out. In most cases, it can be done if you're committed to it.

Dad, when you're willing to budget and spend money on books, teaching tools, eating out, and retreats, you prove to your wife that you are serious about home education.

Your WIFE Needs: YOUR TIME

"There is a time for everything, and a season for every activity under heaven: . . . a time [for a homeschooling mom] to weep and a time to laugh, . . . a time to search and a time to give up, a time to keep and a time to throw away."

❖ ECCLESIASTES 3:1-6

I HOPE THIS DOESN'T shock you, but your wife needs time away from the kids . . . and you. Occasionally, she gets to the point that if she doesn't get some peace and quiet, she may end up on *America's Most Wanted.*

Don't take it personally. All moms need time alone, and some more than others.

I can tell when my wife hits that point because she starts to get a tad more cranky than normal. Looking like a caged lioness, she paces back and forth and growls, "I never have time to do what I'd like to get done."

She looks me straight in the eye and asks, "Isn't there somewhere you can take the kids?"

I've half wondered if she doesn't mean the orphanage or the river, but I know by now she only means "take them away."

Being the good husband that I am (and wanting to preserve my life), I load the kids into the van, and we head to Wal-Mart. We browse the toy aisle and get a cookie at the bakery.

When I figure we've spent enough time away and deem it safe to return, we do. You should see the difference that two hours of alone time makes in my wife's demeanor. While we're gone, some sort of miracle takes place. Mrs. Grinch leaves and my sweet, loving wife returns.

She's all smiles, hugs, and kisses and is able to view life once again through unclouded eyes. Even as I write this, I can sense it's time for me to take the kids away, or better yet, send her off with a friend for a couple of hours.

THE GIFT OF TIME

The gift of time is an amazing thing. With it, your wife can relax, plan, focus, and get things done. Without it, your wife will get frustrated, sidetracked, defeated, and worn out. In fact, time is one of the greatest gifts you can give your wife (other than jewelry).

Alice decided to speak her husband's language.

She needs time off to relax, get together with friends, plan, pray, and be intimate with you. When you give her time, your school will run smoother, she will have more patience, your kids will enjoy their mother, and you will get to see your homeschooling wife smile more often.

TIME TO RELAX

Perhaps your wife likes to pretend that she doesn't need time away. Yet after 5,239 hours of being cooped up with five kids, one hyper dog, and a husband, she probably gets a little crazy.

Insist that your wife go out with a friend from time to time. She may protest, saying she doesn't need the break and won't have a good time, but when she returns, with a smile on her face and a lightness in her step, it will be obvious that she did.

Over coffee or a piece of pie, she and her friend can talk about homeschooling problems, kid problems, and husband problems. They can encourage each other to hang in there, pray for each other, and just talk about things that grown-ups talk about.

A night out or a kid-and-husband-vanishing-act pretty much solves the minor episodes of homeschool burnout, but at least once a year she also needs to get away and get her homeschooling batteries recharged.

TIME AWAY

One of the best encouragements for the homeschooling journey is to get your wife together with a group of home-schoolers at a retreat. There is strength in numbers as they listen to one another's struggles and describe what has and hasn't worked for them.

The women learn, laugh, and nod their heads in agreement as they share stories and tips. Together, they pray and worship as an army of women who have chosen to teach their children at home. They stay in a hotel, dine at a leisurely pace, feed their souls, and fellowship with friends.

There are many weekend getaways to choose from that are usually within driving distance. They're not always cheap, and you'll have to watch the kids all by yourself for a couple of days, but it's money and time well spent. Your wife will return recharged, pumped up, and ready to go.

I secretly think part of my wife's enjoyment is knowing that I have the kids all by myself and that I get a taste of what her normal day is like. She doesn't say that, but she laughs a little too loud when I recount all the mishaps that happened while she was away.

Yet some women don't go on retreats because their husbands refuse to watch the kids for that long. I feel ashamed that a man would act that way. That is pure selfishness. Of course, it's not easy to do all the things that our wives do everyday, but remember we're committed to the cause, to our children, and to our wives.

TIME TO PLAN

At least once a summer I give my wife a day or two of planning. No kids, no husband, no distractions. She needs it to plan the upcoming year of school.

She's tried to fit it in with her thousand other chores, but we've found that she needs some concentrated time to pour over the curriculum, the schedule, and books.

We have the luxury of having a family cottage not far from our home, but you might need to send your wife to a hotel, her parents' house, or take the kids on an all-day outing. You'll be surprised by how much she can get done in that time of clear thinking and praying.

There is also much school planning needed day-to-day throughout the year. Some husbands give their wives every Saturday morning to plan for the coming week. It may only take an hour, but again, when your wife doesn't have distractions, she can get a lot done.

Now, I know you may be thinking, "Every Saturday?! When am I supposed to get the things done I need to do . . . and besides, that's when I usually play golf."

Dad, if you're committed to educating your children at home, you'll give your wife the time she needs. If you're not, well, then go ahead and play golf. Just don't be too surprised when your wife and your homeschool come unglued.

TIME WITH GOD

The most important time your wife needs is time alone with God. If she's going to do her job well, she's going to need to stay close to God. It's your job as the lead dog to make sure she has that time. Guard it, like a secret service man guards the president. Keep the kids away, and let her meet with God in peace and without distractions.

If the morning is best for your schedules, get up early, feed the kids breakfast, and clean up the kitchen while your wife spends that time with God.

If evenings work better, then let your wife go to a quiet place and keep the kids away. It doesn't have to be for hours or even an hour; a half hour may be enough.

If you travel or can't find a consistent time, arrange your schedule when possible, and plan to watch the kids. Even

once or twice a week alone with God is better than no time.

Again, I can't overstate the importance of letting your wife spend time with God. Don't believe me? Give it a try and see the transformation in your wife's attitude, endurance, and outlook.

TIME WITH YOU—NO KIDS

Your wife also needs some alone time with you. Back in the old days you used to call it a date. You know, you used to take your not-yet-wife out to a restaurant, a movie, or a walk in the park.

Those were great days. You held hands, stared into each other's eyes, and talked about the future.

After a few years of married life something happened. You quit dating. First, there were the demands of work and raising kids, and then you started homeschooling, and you just kind of ran out of time and got tired.

Maybe you've even convinced yourself that you don't really need dates anymore, that you've outgrown them.

Well, let me say this gently . . . BALONEY!!!

You and your wife need dates like you need air. You need to leave the kids with a babysitter, relative, or an older child, and go out. Hold hands. Look into each other's eyes. Talk.

Think you've forgotten how? Well, it's like riding a bike. Get away from the kids, and it will come back to you.

Don't be surprised or bothered if all your wife wants to talk about is homeschooling and kids. Her mind is bottled up with school stuff, and she wants to talk to her man about it. Just smile and listen.

Trust me on this one. Even if you insist that you don't need date nights—you do!

P.S. Before you proceed to the next chapter, go to your calendar and plan a date night. Surprise your wife by taking care of all the arrangements. Call a babysitter, pick the restaurant (her favorite, not yours), and then let her know what you've done so she can anticipate it.

THE QUESTION

So, Dad, if you want your wife to survive and thrive, then you better give her time. Time to relax, time to socialize, time to plan, time with God, time without you, and time with you. Don't wait until she asks, because she may not.

Take the initiative and insist that she get away for a while, that you and the kids disappear for a few hours, or that you two go out on the town. She may say that she doesn't need it, but you know better.

CHAPTER EIGHT

Your WIFE
Needs: YOUR
UNDERSTANDING

"You husbands [of homeschooling moms] in the same way, live with your wives in an understanding way."

❖ 1 PETER 3:7 NASB

IT WAS FRIDAY. My mind had been brewing all day. We had nothing going on that night, so I was laying plans for some romantic time with my wife. Without getting gory on you, it involved candles, soft music, and . . . other stuff.

The day went by slowly as I anticipated the great night ahead of us. Only one problem: I failed to mention my plans to my homeschooling wife who'd had a typically long and exhausting week.

By the time I was ready for liftoff, she was coming in for a landing.

"I'm whipped," she announced with a sigh. "It sounds so good to go to bed early."

I looked at her, hoping I hadn't heard what she just said. Didn't she know what I had planned?

SETTING THE MOOD

Thinking a little mood setting would do the trick, I tiptoed into the bedroom after the kids were in bed, lit a few candles, and put a romantic CD into the stereo. "Yeah, now we're talking. She can't resist this," I thought, admiring my work.

A few minutes later, she walked into the room, saw the candles, and said, "You're kidding, right?"

My bubble was burst, and I did the only natural thing at the time. I pouted and gave her the silent treatment.

"You're mad at me, aren't you?" she asked.

"Nope. I'm not mad."

"What were you thinking?"

"Nothing," I insisted. "I was just testing to make sure all the candles were working in case of a blackout." She knew

The smile quickly vanished from Tom's face.

that I was upset and tried to make it up to me with little success. My plans were ruined. It was plain to me that she no longer found me attractive or desirable . . . she probably wasn't even as in love with me as I was with her. There was no salvaging the night, so I slunk downstairs and puttered around for a while.

In the morning, my wife apologized, and I tried to pretend I wasn't hurt. She tried to explain that she was just exhausted from the week, but I wasn't buying it. Eventually, we were both mad, and we had a terrible day.

A REVELATION

No kidding—I was really struggling with this until I heard an interview on Focus on the Family Radio. I'm not sure who it was or what the program was about, but the woman said, "I just want my husband to understand that it's nothing about him . . . I'm just tired."

Then it hit me—my wife is just tired. Your wife is tired. All homeschooling moms are tired. That's just the way it is.

I don't have to take it personally or wonder why she doesn't desire me like she used to—she's just tired. Since I'm committed to homeschooling, I better get used to it because she's going to be tired for a long time.

I've found that to enjoy the wife of my youth, I must get her away and let her rest and relax. I have to give her time to get out of the teaching mode and away from the stresses and demands of the day. I have to give her time to refresh herself and remember that she's still my girl even though she homeschools our five children.

Then, the girl with the big smile and sparkling eyes reappears and the fireworks begin.

IT GOES BOTH WAYS

Now, you might be saying, "Yeah, well I'm not the senti-mental mushy guy you are, Todd. I don't need all that kissin' and squeezin'."

Well, maybe your wife does. Maybe she needs a big kiss and squeeze from her man when he comes home from work. I know you're tired and want to crash on the couch, but this book isn't about what you need, it's about what she needs and equipping her to do the task of homeschooling.

She may need you to tell her how much you love and appreciate her. She might want you to snuggle up with her on the couch and hold her in your strong arms. She might need you to light some candles and put on a soft CD. The key is you have to know your wife.

HOMESCHOOLING CAN DO WEIRD THINGS TO A PERSON

For the first several years of our marriage, my wife kept a spotlessly clean house. Everything had a place, and every-thing was in its place. The books were on their shelves stacked shortest to tallest; toys were arranged neatly in baskets and boxes. The kitchen was clean, the floors glistening, and the carpets had uniform vacuum marks in neat patterns.

Then we started homeschooling, and things changed.

My wife is still a neat person, but now she's a neat person who just can't quite keep up. Now the breakfast dishes sit by the sink at lunchtime, and toys litter every room. At times, walking across the kitchen floor feels like walking across a beach of crunchy seashells, and mountains of laundry fill the hamper waiting to be washed.

Now, let the record show that my wife works hard to keep

up on the housework. It's just that there is no humanly possible way to keep up with it all, and some things just have to go.

For us, it was those neatly crisscrossed vacuum patterns and books stacked shortest to tallest. Fortunately, I'm a slob and hardly notice the difference, but I know for some men a mess is almost more than they can stand.

One dad, who is a self-confessed neat freak, tries to get his wife to run a tighter ship and even offers to teach her how to do so to no avail.

He told me how he had come home from a long day of work and was blown away by the mess and chaos as he walked in the door.

They had dinner, and after the kids were in bed, his wife looked at him and asked, "So what's on TV?"

Without missing a beat, he answered, "Dust."

He laughed when he told me the story. I wanted to slug him.

NOW HEAR THIS!

Your homeschooling wife doesn't need your criticism, she needs your understanding. She needs you to overlook the mess, the piles, and her tiredness.

She needs you to see the incredible load that is hers to bear because, together, you decided to home educate your children.

When you are confronted with an empty closet and no clean shirt to wear, scrounge around and wear a dirty one. When she serves you another bowl of cereal for dinner, smile and enjoy it. And when the dust is thick on the TV, tell your wife to sit down and enjoy the evening while you and the kids do a little serving.

Bill knew from her non-verbal cues that
the kids had been hard that day

LIVE WITH YOUR WIFE IN AN UNDERSTANDING WAY

Whatever your bent, whether you're a hugger, a neat freak, slob, or organizer, you need to adjust for her. You need to be understanding of her day and know, really know, what she needs and doesn't need from you.

It's your job, like the verse says, "to live with your wife in an understanding way."

You may say, "Yeah, but I haven't had a clean pair of underwear in three days, and I can't remember the last time we had a home cooked meal."

My answer to you: Live with your wife in an understanding way.

"Yeah, but you don't understand . . ."

Your Wife Needs: **YOUR UNDERSTANDING**

No, *you* don't understand. Live with your wife in an understanding way. If you are committed to homeschooling your children, then live with your wife in an understanding way! Understand?

CHAPTER NINE

Your WIFE Needs: YOUR APPROVAL

"A cheerful look brings joy to the [homeschooling mom's] heart."

❖ PROVERBS 15:30

UNREALISTIC EXPECTATIONS are a great burden to your homeschooling wife. I continually hear accounts of wives who feel the jarring weight of trying to live up to their husband's unrealistic expectations.

Some men get upset that their children aren't reading at the level they should be or that their seventeen-year-old hasn't quite grasped the concepts of advanced calculus. They offer criticism but not help. They offer plenty of advice but rarely do anything to remedy the situation.

Some husbands expect a spotless house. "After all," they say, "the house is to be a haven in which I can find refuge after a hard day of work." Instead of offering to help, they make comparisons to other people's homes.

Some men want meat and potatoes for dinner—every night. They can't believe they are served pancakes instead. They don't offer to help with the meals, but they serve large portions of disappointment to their wives regularly.

THE LOOK OF DISAPPOINTMENT

Our wives see the disappointment in our eyes. It says to them that they have failed to meet our expectations. We don't necessarily mean to communicate that, but when we raise an eyebrow and frown or say unkind words, we communicate exactly that.

When you express disappointment, your wife often feels as though she has failed, not only in educating the children, but also as a homemaker and wife.

If you think I'm overstating the truth, you're wrong! Most homeschooling moms feel like failures. And the really sad thing is that most of their husbands, including this one, are sometimes the cause of it.

If you find yourself nodding in agreement, then maybe it's time to ask for your wife's forgiveness, and God's as well.

If you need help in this area, stop right now and pray.

THE GREATEST GIFT

Dad, the greatest gift you can give anyone, especially your wife, is your approval. Your wife will feel as if you've handed her the world.

She won't have to worry about trying to educate the children and being superwoman at the same time.

When she tells you how one of the children acted up, don't tell her what she should have done, just tell her that you understand how hard it is.

When you walk in the door and it looks like a surplus store exploded in your house, hug her and empathize with her hard day. Then, get busy and help clean up the mess.

Instead of making your exhausted lover feel guilty for not meeting your needs, pamper her by massaging her feet and rubbing her back (expecting nothing).

Remember, when all is said and done, it won't really matter when your child learned to read, whether the house was always clean or not, or what you had for dinner. What will matter is your relationship with the members of your family.

So relax, gather up all your unrealistic expectations, and toss them in the trash.

Your WIFE Needs: YOUR PRAYERS

"The prayer of a righteous [homeschooling husband] is powerful and effective."

❖ JAMES 5:16

HOMESCHOOLING IS A prayer-sized job. It ranks right up there with moving mountains and parting seas. In fact, it can't be done as God intended it without prayer. I'll bet that your wife already does a lot of praying—homeschooling does that to a person.

But what about you? Are you praying for your wife, your children, and your role in educating your children? Most believers talk about the power of prayer, yet very few do it, even though it's the greatest thing that you can do for another person.

Pray for her. I mean really pray for your wife. You know the kind of prayer you pray when you think you're going to lose your job and you go to God and ask Him to allow you to keep it? Pray with that kind of intensity.

Your homeschooling wife has so many needs each day. The previous chapters prove that. When you fail to pray for your wife and her needs, you are hamstringing her efforts. She just isn't as effective as a teacher or mom when you don't pray for her.

I know one dad who prays over his wife every morning. Before he heads out the door, he places his hands on his wife and prays.

He prays for wisdom, strength, protection, and for supernatural teaching abilities. When he says "Amen" and goes off to work, he has better equipped his wife for the day.

It makes a difference, not only in that woman's day, but also in her husband's day and their affection for each other.

Try it out and see what happens.

ALL DAY LONG

But don't stop there. Keep praying, going to bat for your wife all day long.

Do this: Get a brightly colored post-it note and write the words "Pray for (insert your wife's name)." Then stick the note somewhere you'll see it throughout the day.

Stick it on your phone at work, on your computer monitor, on your dashboard, or in your lunch bucket. All day long, send up prayers on her behalf and on behalf of your children. Ask her what specific concerns you can pray for. She'll probably brush you off, thinking you don't really want to know, but ask her again. If she can't think of any, give her a day or two and ask again.

When she gives you her requests, write them down on your sticky note and pray.

A homeschooling mother's prayer

Then, later, ask her how those things have gone. She will know that you have been praying for her needs, and she will know beyond a shadow of a doubt that you are committed to homeschooling. Together you'll see God answer your prayers. Why? Because God answers prayer.

Now you're not just saying it. You're living it.

Pray for your wife's:

1. strength and endurance
2. wisdom in discipline
3. patience
4. persistence

5. calmness and gentleness
6. discernment and fairness
7. self-discipline
8. deeper relationship with God
9. love in all things
10. inner peace
11. creativity and innovation
12. listening heart
13. sensitivity to the Holy Spirit
14. contentment with circumstances
15. sense of purpose
16. direction
17. love of learning
18. energy and rest
19. selflessness
20. joy

CHAPTER ELEVEN

Your WIFE
Needs: YOUR
SACRIFICE

"Husbands, love your [homeschooling] wives, just as Christ loved the church and gave himself up for her."

❖ EPHESIANS 5:25

THE VERSE ABOVE serves as a constant reminder that being a husband of a homeschooling mom is all about sacrifice. In the same way that Christ gave up everything for you, you in turn must give it all up for your wife. You ought to hold nothing back.

Your time is not yours.

Your money is not yours.

Your comfort and leisure time are not yours.

Your life is not yours.

Your expectations are not yours.

Nothing.

GREAT GIVEAWAYS

All your rights and privileges were given to you to sacrifice for your wife, family, and others. With homeschooling, the sacrifice is even greater. If your family is to make it through homeschooling, then you will have to give up things that you like, things that other men enjoy, and things that you've grown accustomed to and hold on to.

Being a homeschooling husband is a labor of love. When it comes down to it, love is not an option to be chosen; it is a command to be obeyed. You may hate it (I know I do sometimes), but you can't escape the command: (Insert your name), love your homeschooling wife as Christ loved the church and gave Himself up for her.

CAN YOU HAVE IT ALL?

Sometime in the last forty years, men got the idea that they can have it all. They were told that they can have a high-paying, ladder-climbing career, a great home with a freshly painted white picket fence, and a smiling family that feels loved and cared for, all at the same time.

In fact, that has even become a popular message in Christian circles. Unfortunately, it's wrong. The truth is, you can't have it all.

Hold it. Let me rephrase that. You DO have it all!

The investment that you make in the lives of your wife and children has significance that will last for all eternity. Therefore, you have all that truly matters.

The job that you hold, no matter what the position, will one day be held by someone else. The car that you drive will one day be melted down and turned into a toaster. The bank account and investments that you're building will go to someone else or disappear in an investment fund scandal.

Many men are so willing to sacrifice the really good stuff for things that don't matter. They neglect their children, their spouses, and their duty to home, and they selfishly pour their energy into themselves.

Not you though. You're different. You know where you're going and why you're going there. You've chosen a tough path, and still you press on.

You won't be able to achieve the position you always wanted. You won't have the savings account you dreamed about. Your friends won't always see you on the golf course or at the gym. You may not be able to restore the '68 Corvette or have the ChemLawn yard of the year.

But you don't care about that.

You have chosen the best. You have chosen to educate your children at home and invest in your family.

Let others gawk and shake their heads at your "wasted earning potential." They won't understand, but you do and so does God.

You have chosen well. And let me say it again, YOU HAVE IT ALL!!

Don't trade it for anything.

CHAPTER TWELVE

Your Needs: THE TWO BIGGIES

"Let us [homeschooling husbands] hold unswervingly to the hope we profess, for he who promised is faithful. And let us consider how we may spur one another on toward love and good deeds."

❖ HEBREWS 10:23–24

WE'VE SPENT THE LAST eleven chapters talking about the needs of your homeschooling wife. Now, we are going to spend the last chapter talking about two of your needs.

THE PRIMARY RELATIONSHIP

Dad, your single greatest need is to have a growing relationship with God. The bookstore shelves are lined with titles to aid you in that process. They're the books that people buy you on Father's Day and Christmas that you don't often read.

If this need is not met, then the work of the previous chapters can't be accomplished. You can try, but you'll find yourself unable to do all that you need to do. It's like trying to cut a stack of wood with a chainsaw before you pull the cord. You've got the tool but no power. God is the power. Plug in.

The homeschooling mind

Your relationship with God isn't meant to be a burden or a series of steps for reaching "Christian nirvana" as some have tried to make it. It is simply a real, vital relationship between you and God.

A relationship means you communicate and share with each other. You spend time together. Sound simple? It is.

God wants you to come to Him, trust in Him, and rest in Him. He wants you to ask for wisdom and strength, and to depend on Him as if your life depends on it—because it does.

Unfortunately, most of the time we try to go at it alone. We know that we need to lead our family, which is a good thing, and then don't look to God for direction. So we head in the direction that we feel is best, not realizing that it's the wrong direction.

WHAT DOES GOD SAY?

We talked earlier about the reasons behind homeschooling. Instead of listening to me or the authors of some of the books that I suggested, why not see what God says about training your children at home?

Don't know where to begin? Get your Bible. Open it to Ephesians. Read with the eye of a husband of a homeschooling mom.

Read a few verses a day. Pay attention to the things that apply to dads, husbands, and men trying to train their children. Read on your own, with your wife, and/or in a Bible study, and don't be afraid to ask questions and consult commentaries to further your understanding.

Here are a few sections to visit:
Deuteronomy 6
Psalm 34
Psalm 78:1–8
Proverbs
Matthew 7:7–11
Ephesians 5:25–33
Ephesians 6:4
Colossians 3:21
Hebrews 12:4–11

FIND TIME

I know it's hard to find the time, but determine to carve a small chunk of time out of your busy day to spend alone with God. No distractions. It's the time when you "tank up" to do the things that you need to do, including meeting the needs of your wife and family.

Maybe it's in the morning before everyone else gets up, during your lunch break, or after the kids are in bed. During that time, read a few verses from your Bible. Maybe you'd benefit by writing down your prayers and how and when they are answered. Or you could underline the verses that especially struck you. And share verses and prayer requests with your wife. Don't feel like you have to break any world records, just spend at least a few minutes with God.

Remember your time with God doesn't end there. You may not be able to study your Bible at work or kneel down beside your desk, but you can say a quick prayer every time you see your sticky note and during your commute.

Don't think I am trying to initiate another program into your life, because I'm not (none of us has time for another one anyway). Spending time with God is not an activity to check off from your list, like brushing your teeth or eating breakfast. It's just one father spending time with another Father.

IRON SHARPENS IRON

Your second greatest need is for encouragement. Just as your wife needs an encourager, so do you. All of us dads need one and need to be one.

Find another man who will encourage you to love your homeschooling wife. Make sure he's someone who will ask you the tough questions and challenge you to keep on trying. Maybe you can find a group of men who want to lead their families but struggle to do so (you won't have to look hard).

Remember, you don't have to start some sixteen-step-husbands-of-homeschooling-moms program. You don't have to do a Bible study or go through a book (although this book would be a good one to talk through). All you have to do is get together and talk. Talk about how you're doing as husbands, fathers, and men.

Be real. Tell them where you fail and pray for one another. It doesn't have to be a weekly thing. Maybe it's every other week or once a month. Meet together during lunch or before work—just some time that doesn't take you away from your family time.

The important thing is to do it.

A FAMILY MAN COMMERCIAL

Hi there, Dad! Todd Wilson talking at you. You say you want to love your wife and children the way God created you to? You like what you've read here but don't know where to start? You're not sure about getting a bunch of guys together, because it sounds too hard, too vulnerable?

Well, have I got a deal for you.

Every week I send an e-letter to dads all over the country. It's just one dumb old dad encouraging another in the best job there is—fathering. I know you get plenty of e-mails a day vying for your time, trying to sell you the latest, greatest product known to man, but mine is different.

I just want you to live a life with no regrets. Besides, this weekly letter is short, sweet, and real.

So, if this sounds like something you'd like to receive, e-mail me at familyman@bnin.net or visit my Web site at www.familymanweb.com.

Join The HOHM Club
(pronounced HOME)

Please rise. Congratulations! You are an official member of The HOHM Club. Dad, God chose you for the task of being a Husband Of a Homeschooling Mom. You did not choose it; He chose you. It's an incredible job that you have been called to do.

Some men in history were thrown to lions, sawed asunder, or banished. You have received a different trial—that of being married to a homeschooling mom.

Will it ever be easy?

"NO!"

Would it be easier to put your children in school?

"Yes!"

Is that what you want to do?

"No."

Are you committed to home educating your children?

"Yes."

Can you do it?

"Yes."

Can you do it without prayer?

"Not the right way."

Are you the lead dog?

"Grrrrr! Yes, I am."

Do you promise to give your wife the resources she needs to do the job, including time, money, and involvement?

"You bet!"

Will you do dishes, take your family out to eat, and help with the housework?

"Yes sir!"

I can't hear you!

"Yes, sir!!!"

Will you lower your expectations and seek to live with

your wife in an understanding way, even if the most warmth she shows you is to swat a fly from your shoulder?

"Yes, sir!"

Good. Now it's up to you to encourage other HOHMs in this daunting task. You must encourage other dads to love their wives in the way Christ loved the church. You must remind them of all the fundamentals of being a HOHM.

If they slack off, you must get in their face and remind them of this great responsibility.

If you do that, an army of godly men and women will arise. God is counting on you, Dad. Your wife is counting on you. Your children are counting on you. I'm counting on you.

You can do it!

"YES, SIR!!!!!"

Dismissed.

"Reminding dads of what's most important"

About The Author

Todd Wilson is a writer, speaker, and dad. As founder of Familyman Ministries, his passion and mission is to change the world one dad at a time through weekly e-letters to dads, seminars, and books that encourage parents. Todd, his wife Debbie, and their six children make their home in Indiana.

Every dad needs encouragement in fathering. This weekly e-letter is a lighthearted look into the heart of a dad. It is encouraging, funny, and pathetically real. To sign up, send a blank e-mail to familyman@bnin.net or go to **www.familymanweb.com**

If you'd like me to encourage your group, call
574.658.3247
or go to
www.familymanweb.com

"Now that you've read the book, share it with other dads."

HELP!
I'm **Married**
to a **Homeschooling**
MOM

Showing Dads *How to*
Meet the Needs of Their
Homeschooling Wives

TODD WILSON

Familyman ministries
"Reminding dads of what's most important"

Hey Dad,

    I bet you know a lot of homeschoolers. You know what? Every one of them needs this book. It's universal - homeschooling is hard, and it takes a husband and wife committed to the cause. Unfortunately, dads forget that. It's up to us to remind them.
    Will you take it upon yourself to get this book into the hands of at least one other dad who's married to a homeschooling mom? Or why not see if your homeschooling group would buy one for every couple.

You 'da Dad!

Todd

Familyman Ministries
www.familymanweb.com

only
$9⁹⁹
per copy

MOODY
PUBLISHERS

THE NAME YOU CAN TRUST®

HELP! I'M MARRIED TO A HOMESCOOLING MOM TEAM

ACQUIRING EDITOR
Mark Tobey

COPY EDITOR
Ali Childers

BACK COVER COPY
Lisa Cockrel

COVER DESIGN
UDG| DesignWorks

INTERIOR DESIGN
Ragont Design

INTERIOR ILLUSTRATIONS
Todd Wilson

PRINTING AND BINDING
Color House Graphics Inc.

The typeface for the text of this book is
Berkeley